# DAN CHELOTTI

McSWEENEY'S
POETRY SERIES

# MᶜSWEENEY'S

SAN FRANCISCO

www.mcsweeneys.net

Copyright © 2013 Dan Chelotti

Cover art and frontispiece by Ian Huebert

The McSweeney's Poetry Series is edited by Dominic Luxford and Jesse Nathan.

The editors wish to thank Assistant Editor Rachel Z. Arndt, Editorial Interns
Greg J. Griffith, Alex Morris, and Jasmine Dreame Wagner, and copyeditor Britta Ameel.

ISBN: 978-1-938073-39-7

Printed in Michigan by Thomson-Shore

*In memory of Herman Gustaf Duvall*

———————

*For Selma Ruth Chelotti*

TABLE OF CONTENTS

## BALL LIGHTNING

I am looking out over
one of the first real gray
days of autumn listening
to a podcast in which
these two men are talking about
the phenomenon of ball lightning.
I love ball lightning because (still)
no photographic evidence exists.
It was because of ball lightning
that before everyone carried cameras
I carried a camera hoping
someone would ask me why
I was carrying a camera.
No one ever did, but now,
older, I am grateful to find
that my loneliness
accommodates my desire, and not,
as it used to be, vice versa.

## PARTICULAR ICE

The ice writes a memoir
on my window.
I heard the ice.
I remember particular
ice falling in 1996.
The kind of ice
that traps you.
And being trapped
at a friend's house,
I drank fuzzy beer
until I puked off his deck,
my fingers slipping
from the railing. Then,
like now, I saw it coming
but couldn't parse it.
That is the way with ice,
with foxes that walk
out of the forest
and cross the paths
I walk alone,
with rivers, rest stops,
and the smell of someone
I once knew passing
into a life that is not mine.
If I had a river
I would reach it with a stone.

## GRIEVING IN THE MODERN WORLD

When someone died
in ancient times, say,
in a battle, or from
a thorn and the lack
of penicillin, the women
were said to let their hair
down. Their grief freed them.
This custom is lost
but can still be found
in over-edited movies
where women cut their own
hair in fluorescent bathrooms—
the cuts uneven but cute,
striving after Ingrid Bergman
in *For Whom the Bell Tolls*.
Woody Guthrie also spent
a lot of time striving
after Ingrid Bergman.
He kept a broken watch
in his pocket to symbolize
how time stopped when
he saw her. Woody Guthrie
never got to use that line—
but he did, for a time,
save the world. It would
seem fitting to let my
hair down to show how sad
this makes me feel,

but the microwave is
almost finished heating
my dinner, and the news hour
is about to begin.

## MAGIC

The mechanic says
I have a great ear
for cars, but no ear
for music. I don't ask
how he knows
or say the grease
smudges on his hands
look fake. I walk
away like one who
has three hours to kill
in a strange town
walks away. There
is a cemetery in which
I try to ignore
a headache. A phone booth
with a phonebook
but no phone. A corner
store that has only
rumors of ibuprofen.
These things happen
and I always think
the universe will show
me another path.
Why do I expect magic
only when things break down?
I would love a bath—
a bath and a hamburger.

## ON WILLIAMS'S "TO ELSIE"

Today I walked like a rooster
through the pines.
They were all in my way.
I had my headphones in
to spite the birds.
I put it on shuffle
and pushed past
all songs that did not
corroborate my anger.
I felt just, I felt strong.
Then Elsie, flailing
out from behind a tree
and Williams's reedy voice:
*The pure products*
*of America go crazy.*
It is hard to be angry
when Elsie and her big
floppy breasts want
to cuddle. I don't want
to cuddle, I want to walk
and be righteous like a knight
wielding a sword
of wind and a sword of rain.
I do not want to witness
and adjust. O merciful God,
I do not want to drive the car.

1987

If only the moon
would part the clouds
so the melon vender,
bored, would be unable
to leave his stand.
So that I could buy a melon.
He hasn't been there
for ten years, and for that
he was only there
one night. Why
do I remember him?
Why do I fantasize
about buying or not
buying a watermelon?
Why do I remember
the spider outside Sears
on an early winter
day in 1987 when
I am standing
in a supermarket
looking at the fat content
on a bag of chips?
"For God's sake
where do the things
that matter go?"
He hands me a melon
and doesn't answer.
Just grins at the money
in my outstretched hand.

## IDÉE FIXE

I love the squeak
of a trash can
on wheels rolling
through the ether riddled
with the unwritten letters
of those waiting
for a flight from DC
to Boston. No one
listens to the president
on the cable news
because the cord
running from the flat
screen to the coffee-
stained wall reminds
everyone of their father,
how his breath dispersed
as he chopped a dying elm
in early autumn,
how his breath
dispersed the solid air.
Their screens won't
help them, the music
in their ears will only
encourage the nostalgia
that rushes down
on them like a wind
from a mountain
they wouldn't dare climb.

The president says
it is a question
of our humanity.
The janitor ignores
a wrapper—
a distant blast from a turbine
begins like a fax
from God.

## MIGRAINE CURE

The rain says, Listen to Debussy,
go ahead, Debussy will fix you.
But the rain is a liar.
I must listen to Desmond Dekker.
If he were alive, I would buy him
a milkshake and say, Here, Desmond Dekker,
it's malted. He would smile
and tell me to believe in myself
although at times I am
Arjuna on the field of the soul.
I wouldn't understand everything
through his patois
but I'd understand what I'd have to:
the sweetness of the milkshake:
the saltiness of the fry:
we are only alive for a short while.

## FRIENDSHIP

A friend gives a friend
a woodcut that defines
friendship and says that
sometimes the things
that don't need to be said
are the things that need
to be said. It is true:
look at the woman who
climbs the mountain
with an ironing board
strapped to her back.
What is she after?
Should I bend
with the remover to remove
her hat? Interpret
her skull to reveal
the mystery? Reduce
the world to fact?
Or should I simply
embrace the woodcut's
trite smile, and grin
because her linen
is oh so crisp, her head
like a piano on a wire
four stories up.

## AUGURY

The birds have always
been there to point out
the axles of my carousels,
to let the dead know
what I'm up to.
Take the day
I stuffed my car with boxes.
I was very sad. I thought,
If only someone could
remind me how to feel.
I got in, started to drive
and a swallow flew
off the back of my head.
This was terrifying.
It began beating against
the passenger seat window,
screaming. I got out of the car
and nodded, thankful.
Just yesterday my wife
had a great idea for a novel.
It was so great it silenced us.
We were driving past so many goats.
Near the end of the goat field
my wife exclaimed, Look, look.
Goats? No, not goats.
A crane, she said, there in the middle
of the goats. You must write
this book, I said. Why?

Because the crane has come
from the land of the dead
to consecrate your idea.
That's great, she said.
And I nodded, grateful
to be of aid.

## HEADLINE

*Spain to exhume purported*
*grave of García Lorca.*
I don't know how to deal
so I write a young poet
who lives in Spain
and tell her to go
see if the moon
turns away or if she
feels the irrepressible
urge to give up her guitar.
The situation is so loaded
it is everything
it is not. Don't write
about it, I will tell her.
But why am I writing about it?
Why does the white sky
hurt me? Why won't the body
of García Lorca rise up
and fade like an ancient fresco
exposed to the air?

# DEAD GUY PANTS

People used to ask me
to put on
my dead guy pants.
I was fond of them
for a while
but I gave it up
because people began
to expect them on me.
They would say, Hey Dan,
would you? And I would,
partly because I loved them.
I'm over that.
But when the nostalgia weighs
like an overripe grapefruit
I pull on my dead guy pants,
look at lit windows
from great distances,
and list all the reasons
I have to take them off.

## I LOVE YOU, MAX JACOB

Did you see the crow?
It had great import
like an approaching thumb
smeared with ash—
but it wasn't for me.
I was wearing a raincoat,
the Connecticut was high,
the conditions perfect.
We put on our shiny hats.
Do you remember, Max?
What happened
to that day? To you?
I look, but you insist
on your absence.
I tape my eyes open.
It doesn't work.
I love the way my lashes
stick when I peel the tape.
I also love spearmint gum
and the smokestack
out the window but
nothing makes me long
for what isn't there
the way you do, sweet Max.
I keep asking myself
why I expect you to teach me
how to sip from the cup
of trembling. I've asked

everyone: teachers, lovers,
statues—the early morning,
the ghosts of the night.
I get the feeling you are
riding a horse on the beach,
leaning down to those you pass
so they can see your brand
new tooth, the one with
the secret inside.

## TO MY CAT

Whenever I stare at her
I think of Apollinaire's hat.
Then I think of Apollinaire's gas lamps
and his fingernails.
I think of Apollinaire
because my cat can walk
in and out of a circle
without disrupting the integrity
of the circle—a quality
I've always associated
with Apollinaire, falling leaves,
and cranes. I once saw a sandhill crane
cutting through a humid night
like a dragonfly through a yarn factory.
It shook me. It made me
miss my cat and realize
I've never once followed
her down the darker
paths of the wood.
Never directly asked her
if she could help me
rise like a moon
over this world
of fluorescent things.

## I LOVE TO HIT HOME RUNS
## AND RUN AROUND THE BASES

I wish I could eat a hot dog
when I run around the bases.
I wish the loudspeakers
would play Mozart's *Sinfonia*
*Concertante* in E flat
when I run around the bases.
They won't play it. Today's crowds'
version of levity is watching
a man shoot a turkey
in the head from close range.
Watch its head explode
in slow-mo on the big screen.
I wish I could save that turkey
and carry it around with me
as I run around the bases.
I wish I could stop eating
meat, but I am weak,
too weak to hit a home run.
But I know I would love
to hit one as much
as I love eating hot dogs,
but without all the guilt.
It wouldn't even need
to be a walk-off, a solo
shot in the third would be fine,
a low line drive. And
as I hit my home run

and run around the bases,
I would think of turkeys,
their ancient heads bobbing freely
backlit on the horizon
like the final sequence
of *The Seventh Seal,*
AM-dial Mozart blaring
from my trusty handheld.

## FAKE IT

In San Luis Obispo
there is a café
I've never been to,
but I say I have
and no one questions me.
On the wide scale
of lies I tell daily,
this one barely registers.
Pretending to be Catholic
registers. I never say it
out loud, I just nod
quietly and quietly nodding
one's head is the fiercest
kind of lie. I believe in it
the same way I believe
in the stink of a rotting
pig's knuckle in the closet
under the stairs—
the same way
I artfully avoid looking
at the holes I punch
in the walls, or artfully
artfully arrange
my books in the boxes
so if anyone sees they will
see how intelligent I am.
I schlep my books
down this long highway
of mice with a limp so subtle.
So subtle you can almost see it.

## PENITENT DAYS

The days surround us,
pressure us into
thinking there might
not be enough time
to say all we haven't said,
or to take it all back.
We walk purposefully
toward rain, blame
our many imaginary
kingdoms, and never
once risk the receipt
of grace inside them.

## WHITE SUN

Where did you come from, silent partner?
Who drew your hands from the stone?
I was alone and tried to avoid you.
I cut stars
as you cut letters to spell
*white sun, cellophane,*
*I have never been alone.*

# SONGS HEARD FROM THREE WINDOWS

1.
Theodore Roosevelt called
Tolstoy a sexual moral pervert.
This is true. He called Tolstoy
a sexual moral pervert because
of *The Kreutzer Sonata*, a novella
in which the Beethoven sonata
figures prominently, which
suggests that some music
is so powerful it can change
your internal states
into foreign states.
Theodore Roosevelt didn't want
his internal states to change at all.
And this is one reason
he shot at elephants.

2.
Some songs make me want
to be punched in the nose.
When I first realized this
it was revelation:
that torments can become
one's elements, that pain
can effectively belay
the longing that longs to be
inside that lit window on the hill
examining the bedposts.

3.
There is an order
to the clouds I cannot discern.
An order that reaches
out and smacks
me like a fox in the woods
in the beam of my flashlight.
And if the flowers on my desk
aren't watered they will continue
posing questions, they will reconstitute
the desk as an echo
of a single chord.

*If You Travel Far Enough...*


The captain once said
If you travel far enough
you will meet yourself.
Once at a faraway gas station
nametag Phil said,
Hey Billy, how goes the day?
But I am not Billy. Not at all.
A mime at heart,
I said, Like yesterday and
tomorrow, I imagine.
You said it, Phil said.
He flopped a pack
of Camels on the counter
and punched a quick pick.
How's Judy? Good, good.
Going to CJ's this weekend?
Yep. Ciao. Ciao for now.
I always thought if I met
my double I would either
have sex with it or kill it,
not be confused
with it by a gas station attendant.

## THE WHITE HAIR OF WISDOM

Sometimes I am struck by a quiet
that conquers the overcast branches
and "The Lark Ascending" on the radio
and the kale and eggs moving through
my digestive tract and I see coming
toward me rectangular shapes.
I wonder if they are issued
from an invisible vessel anchored
somewhere just outside our atmosphere,
captained by some dead unnamed
relative who always keeps on his lap
his cat, Longfellow. I would like this
explanation, but there is no explanation.
I do have a single white hair that grows
just left of the center of my forehead,
and when I pluck it, or a hairdresser
nips it, it seems the shapes
don't come as often. I don't like it
when this happens. I want my shapes.
I want to lean back in the swirling
black orphic infinitudes
with a jar of peanut butter, a spoon,
and a tall glass of 2%. I want to spin
my white hair of wisdom around
a finger as they come, my shapes,
my beloved slices of flying white bread.

## LION

When I come home
there is a lion waiting.
It is not haggard.
You cannot see ribs jutting
out beneath the edge
of a ragged mane.
I'd say the lion is perfectly healthy
but toy-soldier small.
When I draw close
it roars like hell,
postures to nibble my finger.
I don't understand
what it's doing in my world
of ketchup smeared paper plates
and dollar scratch tickets,
of toothpaste and gin.
Its little roars are no louder
than crumpling a post-it note.
I can't bring myself to kill it
or put it outside.
At night sometimes
I think I can hear it
purring in the kitchen,
and during the brief
flashes of clarity
that precede sleep,
I know that it loves me,
that it is only wanting

to protect me,
that, while terribly
insufficient, it will take
on whatever darkness may come.

## SCREAMS

A woman once dropped
a toothpick bridge.
This was an excellent
reason to scream
but she didn't.
She kneeled over it,
silent. I wish I could
stare at something
the way she stared
at that broken bridge.
Instead, I don't know
why I make the decisions
I make or why I often
sit on my head
wondering if I care.
Should I? The man upstairs
who screams
at the sports games
says I should.
Says he is at the thirty,
says the twenty, the ten.
Says, Don't worry,
no one ever does
what they want to do.

## PEOPLE POEM

People intend to write letters, terrible letters. They used to not send them, now they don't write them. Terrible people. People are quite often terrible. Or kind. Or mean to be kind. At airports they mean to say Hi, but don't. They intend to be friendly but instead have ideas. People do not intend to have ideas. Ideas make people walk into walls, into bookstores. Bookstores make people want to write books and go places. People hold signs over their heads at airports, signs naming who should be getting off the plane, but they are not getting off the plane. People used to get off planes and meet people who held signs for them and sometimes they carried books and sometimes they meant to say Hi, but didn't. Now there aren't any people left to hold the signs.

Yes, there are. People don't intend to be terrible to one another, to make things up like I just did. They want to disappear. People want to disappear but people don't know the first thing about disappearing. People love to watch people and not be watched back. Sometimes a turtle makes its way across the floor—a turtle makes its way across the floor with great purpose, but people never see it.

## THE SHEEP OF POWER

I think about kneeling
on my hardwood floor
to hurt for as long
as possible. My mind
fills with a regret
so cathartic and quiet
it brings the seer
of my lineage to bear:
shearing a sheep,
Amelia hums
until I notice
her song isn't a song
but a mandala wheeling
around her enormous head,
and above her enormous head:
the cosmos, and above
the cosmos: the one,
the holy sheep.

## ODE TO HEPHAESTUS, THE BLACKSMITH WHO MAKES LIGHTNING BOLTS AND IS MARRIED TO APHRODITE BUT IS UGLY

Craving a smoke
in the half-assembled
world, I rely on Hephaestus.
When I fake a limp
coming out of a handicapped
bathroom stall, I think
of Hephaestus.
When I see an injured crow,
when I check the tire pressure,
when I hold a book
over the recycling bin
debating whether I'll ever
read it again...
I put it back.
Not because I will
or won't read it
but because of Hephaestus,
the way he bears down
on white metal.
I see his eyes above the weld
and feel better
about not smoking,
about circuitously walking
toward an injured crow
with a tire iron called Mercy.

RERUNS


A guilty man on television says
the earth is a screaming
whore who needs to be gagged.
So gag. Shut her up
with a mud shot. A junk shot.
It's so erotic. Like light falling
hard on the jetty, like chunks
of charred bone dropping
from a plastic container,
I try to mean more than I can.
A man rips by
on a motorcycle.
I hope he falls off.
I say that. I really say that as
I watch men
set fire to the ocean
because it should be
metaphor, but it isn't.
There are no metaphors, just turtles—
turtles and the fists
that fall on tables like
plastic deities with small plastic
dictums: make it
stop. But it doesn't stop,
of course not.
We stuff a giant
pill into the hole and watch
reruns until we forget
the name of our anger.

## THAT'S MATHEMATICS

You unearth a torpedo
and go home. You microwave
a tortoise shell
to see if it sparks.
You take a nice warm bath,
and that's mathematics,
the last train
window-wave on the night
even the frost covered
its face with its cowl.
Why hesitate to jump up
with your flask and pour
some blood on the fire?
I'm suggesting there is a monk
pointing a spear
at the moon, his left hand
trembling because he is the one
who holds the cup that trembles,
because he is the one
who holds the trembling cup.

## A PERFECTLY GOOD OTTOMAN

I've read heaven
is half-finished, overcrowded.
That in heaven
overcoated angels
scurry to file forms
for another lost soul.
I've read heaven
is nothing but
the long walk to hell
and hell nothing
but the long walk to heaven.
I've heard the light
is blinding,
that everyone
who makes it is
in fabulous shape.
I always think
about heaven when I
am at the dump.
The birds that are
supposed to travel
freely between
the land of the living
and the dead really
like the dump.
The men who work
here never say much
and let me linger.

I put a perfectly
good ottoman
in the trunk of my car.
It would be just fine
if when we die
we all become
giant tube worms.

## WALT WHITMAN'S SWEATER

When I put it on
I feel the chuff of daylight
pressing on my back,
speeding me to glide
between the mighty orbs
of our Milky Way's
hem and haw. I
barely even notice
that I forgot to remove
the tag, and the cardboard
cuts into the flesh
of my chest,
that sweet barrel
of wine which I roll
from place to place,
asking you to drink
where I have been,
to gather up what is not
as equally as what is.
Hawk. Moon. Blue truck.
I tuck you all
into the sleeves
which seem too tight
but you will fit.
I will rub honey on your lips
and you will know
what sweetness is.
Hawk. Moon. Blue truck.

Street lamp. Moon. Pharmacy.
Sweater. Cat. Moon.
Pharmacy. Tree.
Tree with a bear in it.

## THE ORCHARD

When we pull through
the great iron gates:
half-eaten pears everywhere.
We drive to the circle
where there are no pears.
My friends step into the circle.
I stay in the car.
No way, no way—
but they make me.
The surrounding hills
shattered by blossoms,
the hut approaching,
the door
plastered with yellowed newspaper
opening. A velvet couch.
We have a new Siamese,
says a voice. Or do you prefer
a French? The French are very good
this year. One friend jumps
and follows the finger.
They all fall. I'm last.
I have just the thing, it says.
How does it know?
I see my friends returning,
eating their pears in silence.

# FOOD COURT

While sitting in the food court
outside the theater, I went
through my wife's bag
and found she carries
a map of London.
She went through my wallet
and found a picture
of my grandmother sitting
on her front steps as a child.
I completely forgot
it was there, though at one time
it was important enough.

The local tribe severed the heads
of the invaders' horses, bleached
and lined the road with them.
It was their hope to ward off
their extinction by doing so.
It is common for fast food
restaurants to put so much ice
in their vampire collector cups
you barely get any soda.
My wife and I talked about
how we will care
for each other when
our memories dissolve,
about how we will find
a way to live in London
before we die.

## POEM AGAINST THE MOON

I draw a line between the streetlight
and the only star, but then the moon
comes round the corner and I'm like,
Hey, Big Fat Moon, why are you always
intruding? It's just like you
to interrupt as I begin
an anaphoric string that features
a streetlight shining through a parked car
onto a pile of rodents. Dammit, Moon!
I have had enough of you.
I will write about her lips!
I will write about her lips
and you won't get to feather them
with your embrace, no you won't.
And you won't get to nest angelic
into her hair, but I will.
I will skip out of time and mad
through the fields of Abraham,
but you won't paint me red.
I am already red.
Moon, I will outdo you.

# THE LIFE OF THE PARTY

I once walked for an entire beach
without seeing a single bird—
it was hilarious, which means sad
with the right pinch of terrifying—
and I kept walking. I kept walking
because although you may think
the life of the party is at the center
of the party, the life is not. The life walks,
not simply around or through the party,
but toward a horizon that only he sees.
All the others are asking each other,
Where is life taking us?
They don't know. They reach out
and pinch the IKEA drapes. They stab
at salsa, but there is nothing for them.
Their life is with me, the life of the party,
who has decided not to join them.

# THE UNBEARABLE AGAIN

It takes twenty years
to sufficiently translate
horror into nostalgia.
Even those who are
horrified by the kitsch
commemorating
the death of x
begin to long.
They revolt
against the dark well
of the past like a plant
in the trunk of a car.
They can't help it.
Twenty years
is not enough time
to explain anything
to anyone.
They stand in front
of churches and remember
the three-dimensional world.
An orange on a wall,
a duck on a mirror,
a mannequin
(it was a mannequin)
thrown from a balcony.

# HELL

A sudden heart attack? An accident?
I can't decide. When I die,
I usually die slowly. This morning:
a quick swerve to blackness.
It was refreshing for a minute
but then I thought of hell.
Driving past prisons
my parents would say in unison,
Who lives there? I would yell,
That's where the bad guys live!
And then they go to hell,
a place underground where dead souls
writhe in pain orgies,
a place ruled by the Lord of Darkness
as played by Tim Curry in *Legend*,
a movie in which darkness
consumes everything.
It scared me so much
I wanted to become the Lord of Darkness
so I could capture pretty girls
and make them wear black dresses.
It was all very erotic in a prepubescent way,
and much better than becoming
a tree of pain at which ravenous birds
ripped my scabrous and pus-ridden flesh.
This is what I did this morning,
a breakfast sandwich in hand.

# THE MAN IN ME

I have a little Pavarotti inside me.
Noticed him while I was brushing
my teeth this evening.
Noticed how I pull apart
my heart's true desires
to spite him.
This was upsetting.
What is the matter
with the world? I ask,
and know the question
itself is false. The little Pavarotti
smoking anisette cigars in my soul
gestures and says, Don't worry, kiddo.
No one really gives a shit
anyway. And because
for a moment there
is nothing more truthful at hand,
I do not enjoy reading
about baseball on the internet.

## THE GIANTESS IS COMING

I wish I had an apartment
in a dusty Italian villa
and a whistle to call
my donkey to me.
When I list
the things I want,
I list a donkey.
It's honest
but it's not honest.
If I owned a donkey
I would feel sad.
For the donkey, for me.
I don't really want
the things I want.
I am able to admit this
in public spaces,
but in private, when
it matters, a recently
tanned twelve-foot
woman with styrofoam eyes
says, Here, here.
Come on home...
I've something to show you.

## MARRIAGE

My eyebrows could grow
so long they strangle
my descendents,
go for a nice walk,
and sit on their graves.
My eyebrows could tell
the passersby
how preferable it is
to drown when the moon
is so full you can't tell if it's full.
I hope for all this
with my hand in my wife's hair.

## STARING AT A WOODCUT ELEPHANT

I've always felt that when you cut into a tree, the newly bared
wood should be warm, and if in winter, it should steam the way a
kettle slowly disappears into the snow.

I should mention the city.

A whole group of men I know likes to sit around and talk about
their pasts. I am supposed to hold myself back. I hate finishing
anything, and this is why I love them. When it comes down to it,
the people I like the most are those who get up early one morning
for no particular reason and catch a deer sniffing around their
outdoor toy train setup.

I believe the dead are around. Just around. When we approach
a meter with a handful of quarters, ready to pay, and find that
someone has overpaid an hour, a small exclamation escapes us, a
little mumble unheard by our fellow pedestrian. This is how we
feed the dead.

## STILL LIFE ON A SCROLLING BACKGROUND

I like to make things happen.
I kick at snow banks thinking
if I disperse them the sun
will have a better chance.
I run into the resting flock.
When someone expects
me to say something,
I pause for a second longer than
expected. I want people to
lean. To lean toward me the way
people lean toward
the finish.

*

I like to think I am
receptive. That I can include
everything. I used to think
this wasn't possible
but then I drank from the cup,
trembled, and was cleansed.
The secret to including everything
is to intricately divide your mind
and then, all of a sudden,
undivide it.

*

I look to the left.
I love looking to the left.
Even when there isn't a window
on my left, I build a wall
just to put one there,
and through the window
I put a helluva landscape,
gorgeous, barren,
termites in the trees,
and in the forefront,
a rat writhing in its trap.
I almost never look
at the rat, trying to follow
the old alchemist's rule:
When stirring the lead into
the mixture, do not think
of a white panther—
I look away.
Stacks beyond stacks of phosphorous.
No, they are moving.
They are waves.

## THE RED STATION

I knock on the door
and say the word.
She lets me pass,
offers a cigarette,
a drink. Who is this
woman? Who am I
waiting for? She
stares at the coffee
table, I stare at her
shoes. He'll be here
soon, she says. This
isn't a doctor's office
but you can tell
yourself it is
if it will make you
feel better.
It's not a whorehouse.
I am not waiting
for drugs. I can't
quite make out
the sound coming
from a nearby room—
someone beating
a dog? An airplane
somewhere overhead.
Children circling
a cracked hydrant.
No one comes in

but a change comes
over her. He's here,
she says. You can go
in now.

## FATHERING

Don't bother
to notice the light
that makes you plunge
your hand in the sand.
You might find
a word you don't want
to find. It will find you
eventually, like I found
you eventually,
but it was too late
in the evening,
you had to get home,
tend to the roast
and your table
of contents. You
left me standing
under a lamp post.
I am always standing
under a lamp post,
even when I am not.
I use a miniature
compass to find
the northmost fountain,
the one by which
I spend my nights
waiting, the one
you told me
to wait by.

Sometimes when the moon
finds its way
through branches
I find a way back
to the street you paved.
You nod, whisper,
Good to see you.
Get on home with yourself.
Say hello to the rest
of the ghosts.
Say hello to the rest
of the ghosts.

# REHEARSING *LEAR* IN THE REARVIEW MIRROR

The air shatters autumn's
frost as I wait scraperless
to drive through the elms
that died from a legendary
disease that snuck
its hand through the kitchen window
and stole them. I wait
as the windshield warms
and stare at pigeons
circling a still-lit
electric lamp. I feel my grammar
center about me. I whisper
  *Allow not nature more than nature needs,*
and bite into a chocolate croissant
with corporate ferocity.
A certain beetle is coming
to destroy our maples.
By 2035 there will be no trees
and we will have to clean
the world by hand. I can't
help but feel responsible
for the acme of it all.
Like gauze stuck to a wound
I must marvel at the bridge as I sweep
the fallen leaves and
collect the last of the asters.
(I must buy a scraper.)
The rakes drag

across the earth
echoing with a particular want,
a deep ache for a silence
so thorough it will bury
all portable electronic devices.
I don't want to be held.
I want to dive into a pool full
of early twentieth-century pornography
while all the ghosts sing Brahms's
*Liebeslieder* waltzes. Instead, a swan
attaches itself to a park ranger
and refuses its mate.
I watch from a corner,
tired, hungry for something more
than a chocolate croissant.
Centuries will come and pass
with clouds tracing paths
for the mind to wage its battles on.
The frost will finally peel back
and reveal the day in all its grace.
The grace, it is said, that will
fool with us all, that will grow.

## A PIECE OF MUSIC THAT SOUNDS
## LIKE SORROW IS NOT REAL SORROW

I want to do nothing but imitate
the voices of others sometimes
I want to do nothing but imitate
the last thing I've read or the song
I've just heard so much so I wonder
if I am anything at all
like Piotr Sommer or Lisa Jarnot
whose books are the first books I saw
just now on the shelf next to my desk
which belonged to my great
grandmother who complained
before she died about all the fucking
in the romance novels my mother
would bring her, about how she used
to put *candles* on the Christmas
trees to risk beauty—that someone should
bring beauty back to the world
or the world might give up
but she didn't really say any of this
except for the thing about the fucking—

## NOVEMBER

The cheap plastic pumpkins
turn into cheap plastic
turkeys and all is renewed.
I walk home from the grocer
with a bag of produce that will rot
on the countertop
as I run to neon-lit chain restaurants.
The days turn like weak sonnets,
cheap and predictable, built
for realization but composed
by the hands of a less-than god
for a globe of less-than believers.
Occasionally in the midst
of the gray-black plenitude
I daydream about rockstardom
to still, momentarily, the death-smile
in the wind. I stand in leather
in front of Cleveland.
I am at the center of all things
turning, all things passing.
I was put here
to put my fist in the air
and thank you
for coming out on a cold Tuesday night.
Thank you, Cleveland.

## GRACE

I received communion once in my life.
I pull a rusted revolver from a lake.
Above us, a passenger jet points
out just how transparent the sky is.
This mark on your forehead.
This row of potatoes.

## REVEAL YOUR COUPON!

Reveal your headstone
by pulling
on this gold lamé rope!
Reveal yourself
to your priest,
your lover,
the floor on which
you push so hard.
It is hard! It will give!
In Postojna it did give
and a man
found the second largest
system of caves
in all Slovenia!
His cow went first.
He clung to her tail,
trusting her eyes.
Think: any day now
you could be
like this man.
Put your coupon
in your wallet
and try not to die
on the way down!

## ANNUAL PERCENTAGE RATE

Sometimes I think about Frank O'Hara
but most of the time
I think about paying
the bills. I find myself
saying *c'est la guerre*
against my will—
I say it to my mother
even though she doesn't
know the expression.
I pass a particularly
leafless tree and
boom, *c'est la guerre.*
Debt frees me
to be an incorrigible
asshole. I want to be
an incorrigible asshole
more than I would like
to admit. Because
I don't like to admit
this, I think of Frank
O'Hara and the way
he almost made
it through his whole
life without using
cherry blossoms
in a poem
but finally couldn't
stop himself.

This makes me feel
better. It makes me think
numbers are just people
trapped in the rain without
umbrellas—that,
though I fear them,
I should let them in.

# FESTIVAL OF SAINT ROCCO

The plastic clown faces
have targets for tongues
and when hit correctly
laugh with such static
it is impossible to hear
the children in line
for The Cobra lunging
at each other. The left
incisor of the man
running the machine
has gone missing again
(and again),
he wants to be inside
the orange fence
where the fathers lean
back in their laughter,
and leaning back
in their laughter
create kinder
sightlines for Rocco
who blesses them,
open sores and all.

## THOUGHTS OVER FOREIGN SANDWICH

My Swedish uncle,
visiting, cooed to me
in Swedish, and I looked
at him then like I would look
at an elderly contortionist.
If I could have a new name
I would be Per.
And being Per, I would
adore calculus.
But dammit,
I don't love calculus,
I don't even know
what calculus is.
I just know that soon
my desk will look
out upon a different
moon, and I will say
what Juan Gris said,
My desk is a trap
into which I fall—
hands first.

## THIS RATE OF EXCHANGE

When someone flinches, I bring up God. I have a friend who
never flinches.

She speaks of her calculations exactly three hours a
day. When I ask why she is particular, she comments on
the weather.

It's not at all different from the times I stare at the subway wall
because it disappears every ten minutes, as precise, if not more,
than the algorithms of my friend.

I say to her "There is an old woman's face in a knot on that tree,
there is an old woman's face behind the old woman's face, and
behind her face there is an elm."

I say "Confessionals didn't exist until the seventeenth
century." I say "It's alright, you should get some sleep. You're
tired." Sometimes I hear her nod consent before she hangs up
the phone.

Just yesterday, a band was playing on the platform. A woman
began crying, dropped her pennies in the trumpeter's hat.
I wanted to ask her why, to put my hand on her back and say,
"There, there, it's only a little while now." I didn't.

She said "The D will take you to Riverside."

# DIAMOND

A baby arduously drags
herself across the rug
to touch the light
reflecting off the Plexiglas
of the entertainment center.
When I pick her up with an
*Enough is enough,* she screams,
and in her scream, I hear
Diamond! Diamond! Diamond!
I never really understood
why people kill people
over diamonds until I bought
a diamond. The seller said
Here, look through the gem scope.
I did, and the earth
and the weight of earth
pressed down on my forehead.
I pushed it into my forehead
and thought its diamond thoughts,
its long silence, its emptiness.
I would kill for it, I said.
I know, it said.

# TRUE STORY

Sartre said that cigarettes
are an aid to perception—
that, when viewing a vista
from the top of a mountain,
cigarettes help the perceiver
breathe in the landscape,
breathe out the landscape.
This is total bullshit
and at the same time totally true
like the story of the monkey
who could climb anything
in the world, but when confronted
by a ladder, sat confounded
because it was in a story
and the teller had forgotten
to describe the ladder adequately.
This is a great problem with stories
and my great grandfather knew this.
He was a sheriff in the Dakotas
and once was cornered in a canyon
by a crew of cattle rustlers.
Because of my ancestor's ability
to describe exactly what he needed,
six Canadian Mounties rode
across the border to his aid.
My ancestor is legendary
to me, and I lament
the lack of him in the world. Some people

say he died earlier
than he should have because
he was a smoker. This is true
but at the same time total bullshit.
The man could balance a frog
on the tip of a pen.

## DAY LATER SUSHI

When I open the fridge
I smell it lurking
in the back. I must wait
for lunch so as to not
be wasteful. Until then
its smell will haunt me
and I won't be able
to be sad. I will
watch a sad movie
to provoke myself
but I won't get through it.
My cartoon bubbles
will stay empty and lodged
right behind my frontal lobe.
My erasers will wear down,
make my mouth
taste like metal.
The morning will expire
and I will stare
out the window
at the empty hummingbird feeder
with a spicy yellowtail
roll in my mouth,
knowing that I should
fill the feeder,
that it would bring me joy.

## WATCH

Because people cannot
fully see what they love,
they wear watches.
I don't own a watch
but I love thinking about
owning a watch. Actually
buying the watch is what thrills
me most. I walk into the shop
and a man approaches.
He says I will be pleased.
I am pleased. I don the watch,
I look at the watch and am comforted.
This is not the kind of comfort
one feels when taking a warm bath
after a day of shoveling manure,
not even close. Anyway, bottom line:
I can rarely ever see anything—
even when it's nothing, nothing,
just concentrating on the road,
on the wall, on the picture
right in front of me
of Allen Ginsberg in the rain.
And it breaks my heart a little
that I can't tell you about it,
that it is my mystery:
the shadowy but convincing
lie that glues the trees to the cement.

## THE REAL WORK

When the phone rings,
even in the middle of
a sandwich, I feel obliged
to answer. I see
a single vestigial board
of what was
a treehouse. Several
tires propped
against the base.
I don't climb the tree.
A lone man in a dinghy
eyes the horizon
and leaves the bay behind.
The Galaxies that fly
over my house
shake my house.
I pause mid-sentence,
let them pass, know the bells
that ring don't ring
loud enough. Our gravity is leaking
into another dimension—

## SHORE LEAVE

I must acquire a flute
to put the golem to sleep.
If I do not have the flute
the golem will not fall asleep
and will kill me.
I will not figure this out.
But as I try
my father lifts weights
and tells me about God.
God, I learn, is very big
but also very small.
This is important.
It makes me say things like,
Oh how I want to learn every name
of every flower! But because
I don't know the name of every flower
I fear things. I fear that God
is a pixilated man like me
walking with his head down
through a forest to a battle
he does not and will not
understand until, years later,
he finds the complete game guide
in a buck store bargain bin,
and attempts to plug it all back in.

# SPENSERIANA

Let's go get a burrito and debate
our favorite pasta shapes
as the crenellated bank
across the way catches the sun.
The late sun, the one that
holds hands with the older trees.
We're not the kind
to exclaim at beauty, so we don't
do anything but notice,
and noticing, shift our conversation
accordingly, to the color
of the capes the Romantics
wore when they flew.
It used to be a walk along the Thames
and boom—pixies frolicking.
Now we walk the strip mall
and attribute strip mall
corner cyclones to . . . to whom?

# THE BOSTON COMMON AT TWILIGHT

When it is snowing
on the Boston Common at twilight
it is the center of the world.
It is not Boston at all,
it is someplace else entirely.
When in New York: New York—
Chicago: Chicago. But in Boston
I am anywhere but Boston.
This is a blessing in that I can transport
myself to anywhere on earth, a curse
in that I am never where I am.
It causes my good friends to say,
Hey, where are you right now?
I am in Germany. I am Paracelsus.
Look at these trees, I am saying—
look at the order a guy can give
to this world of unnamed things.

## SLOW DANCE

I used to hate most
everyone but now
I want to slow dance
with everyone.
In sixth grade I learned
to say *everyone*
not *everybody*
when a teacher looked
teacherly enough,
which means head
slightly bowed.
If she had been wearing glasses
she would have been looking
over them. Power
is a terrible thing
and is what I desired
when I used to hate
everyone. It was like I had
this big binky,
I didn't want
to be separated
from my binky.
It was comforting,
it said I didn't
have to slow dance
with anyone.
So when I look at you sternly,
head slightly bowed,

know that I mean no
*tsk tsk*. I am
too nervous to say
our love is burning
in some distant hall.
That we should go there now.

X

When the continents saw the earth
was eye-shaped they started drifting
apart. I fell in love. I danced again.
Horses fell from the ramparts.
I asked if escape was possible, and you shook your head.
I was four, there were cobwebs, a loading dock—
your nostrils flared. The soles of my sneakers
fought against the pavement.
The train pushed off and I cried.
I don't want to say anything about war.
One stone leaves the hand.
I cower and pat myself on the back.
Leaflets drop from the sky.
I look for God, scratch your grave with my thumbnail,
and there is another cave to paint.
All of this to say I love the salt,
I love the man who sits in the rain,
the small hand that seeks the lever,
the lever that shows the wall is a door.
I love those who forget the names of the trees,
those who pray to God for new dishwashers,
those who wear watches on the subway—
I love the bombs that replace the earth with earth,
I love those who sit silent in automobiles.
I am much shorter than I should be.
I am tall enough to dance. I am tall enough
to recite the name of every flower.
I cut the match heads from the matches

and drop them in the river.
I lose faith, I remember
loving mica among the waves.
I love mothers, sons, daughters.
And father, when you get there—
say I will kneel
as the sun forgives the water
                    for being so cold.

ACKNOWLEDGMENTS


Thank you to the editors of the following journals in which many of the poems in this book have appeared, often in earlier forms: *Bateau, Country Music, Court Green, Fence, Gulf Coast, Handsome, Kulture Vulture, North American Review, notnostrums, Past Simple, Poets for Living Waters, Barrelhouse, jubilat,* and *Tarpaulin Sky.*

Poems from this book also appeared in the chapbook *The Eights* (National Poetry Society of America, 2006).

"Magic" is for Rob, "Still Life on a Scrolling Background" is for Dara, "The White Hair of Wisdom" is for Ian, "The Life of the Party" is to Layla, "Shore Leave" is for Brandon, and "x" is for Kim.

\*

Thank you to all the family, friends, teachers, students, and editors who have supported and pushed me through the years.

Thank you to the teachers and the friends I made at the Colrain Poetry Manuscript Conference.

Special thanks to Matthew Zapruder, Dottie Lasky, Gary Shteyngart, James Tate, Dara Wier, and Peter Gizzi.

Special thanks to Jesse Nathan and Dominic Luxford for challenging me and pushing me to make this book what it is.

Special thanks to J Johnson and Lori Shine, to the Toccis, to Rob Lynch.

Special thanks to Tom Cerasulo and his Aunt Stella, Bob King, Cristina Canales, and Annette Ziomek.

Special thanks to Pat and John Coderre, and to Lillian Duvall. And to Andrew, Kim, and Layla Morgan.

And most special thanks to Kismet Al-Hussaini for seven years of partnership and friendship.

I could not have done this without you.

Cheers.

## ABOUT THE AUTHOR

Dan Chelotti is the author of a chapbook, *The Eights* (Poetry Society of America, 2006), which was selected by Yusef Komunyakaa for the PSA's National Chapbook Fellowship. His poems and reviews have appeared in *Fence, Boston Review, Gulf Coast, Kenyon Review Online*, and many other magazines, and they've been anthologized in *State of the Union* (Wave, 2008) and in *Free Verse*'s "New Voices from New England Supplement." He has an MFA from the University of Massachusetts-Amherst, and has worked as an Assistant Managing Editor for Verse Press. Chelotti is an Assistant Professor of English at Elms College in western Massachusetts.

# THE MᶜSWEENEY'S POETRY SERIES